MVS JCL Utilities

Quick Reference

Second Edition

Robert Wingate

ISBN 978-1500291365

Disclaimer

The contents of this book are based upon the author's personal experience. All of the information in this book should be used at your own risk.

Copyright

The contents of this book may not be copied in whole, or in part, without the explicit written permission of the author. The contents are intended for personal use only. Secondary distribution for gain is not allowed. Any alteration of the contents is absolutely forbidden.

ISBN-13: 978-1500291365
ISBN-10: 1500291366

Contents

OVERVIEW
Purpose

This book includes sample Job Control Language (JCL) code to accomplish many routine file operations using the MVS utility programs. The objectives are to provide ready reference material for the most common utility programs, and to encourage their use. Both these objectives should contribute to programmer productivity by minimizing or eliminating custom programming for simple, routine operations.

This second edition includes more examples, particularly for the SYNCSORT utility, as well as a couple of the IEB utilities.

Additional Resources

This document is not intended to be a training guide. For more detailed information on JCL, consult these excellent references:

z/OS JCL, 5th Edition by Gary Brown

MVS JCL, 2nd Edition by Doug Lowe

Murach's OS/390 and z/OS JCL by Raul Menendez and Doug Lowe

IDCAMS

Copying a Sequential Dataset

IDCAMS is a very versatile utility. You can use it to copy files, but be forewarned **that if you get an error (such as a B37 ABEND), the new file will still get written** – regardless of the (NEW, CATLG, DELETE) file disposition. Since this is usually not what you want to happen, you should, always check the return codes from IDCAMS to ensure everything worked as intended.

```
//JOB00101 JOB (ACCTCODE),'NAME',
//   CLASS=A,MSGCLASS=A,NOTIFY=USERID
//*
//***********************************************
***
//* IDCAMS TO COPY A DATA SET
//***********************************************
***
//*
//STEP1     EXEC PGM=IDCAMS
//SYSPRINT  DD SYSOUT=*
//SYSUDUMP  DD SYSOUT=*
//FILEIN    DD DSN=DSNAME.TEST.FILE,DISP=SHR
//FILEOUT   DD DSN=DSNAME.TEST.FILE2,
//             DISP=(NEW,CATLG,DELETE),
//             UNIT=SYSDA,
//             SPACE=(TRK,(5,5),RLSE),
//             RECFM=FB,LRECL=4096,BLKSIZE=4096
//SYSIN     DD *
 REPRO INFILE (FILEIN) OUTFILE (FILEOUT)
/*
//
```

Copying a Specified Number of Records

Use the **COUNT** parameter to specify a limited number of records to copy from a source file. This can be useful when you want to create test data from a production file, or when you simply want to determine the contents of a file. The following example writes the first 500 records of the input file to an output file.

```
//JOB00101 JOB (ACCTCODE),'NAME',
//    CLASS=A,NOTIFY=USERID,MSGCLASS=A
//*
//************************************************
**
//*   COPY A FILE, BUT STOP AFTER XX RECORDS.
//************************************************
***
//*
//STEP1     EXEC PGM=IDCAMS
//FILEIN    DD DSN=DSNAME.TEST.FILE1,
//             DISP=SHR
//FILEOUT   DD DSN=DSNAME.TEST.FILE2,
//             DISP=(NEW,CATLG,DELETE),
//             UNIT=SYSDA,
//             SPACE=(TRK,(5,5),RLSE),
//
RECFM=FB,LRECL=80,BLKSIZE=0,DSORG=PS
//SYSIN     DD *
     REPRO  INFILE(FILEIN)    -
            OUTFILE(FILEOUT) -
            COUNT  (500)
//SYSPRINT  DD SYSOUT=*
//SYSUDUMP  DD SYSOUT=*
//
```

Skipping a Specified Number of Records

Use the **SKIP** parameter when you want to omit a number of records from a file. You would find this useful if you know precisely how many records you want to omit. For example, you may need to strip some records from a file that is too big to edit online. You can create a smaller output file by skipping over some older records at the front of the file. NOTE: You can use the **SKIP** and **COUNT** parameters together. For example, you can skip the first 1,000 records and then write the next 500 by also including a **COUNT (500)** clause.

```
//JOB00101 JOB (ACCTCODE),'NAME',
//    CLASS=A,NOTIFY=USERID,MSGCLASS=A
//*
//***********************************************
***
//* COPY A FILE, BUT SKIP XX RECORDS.
//***********************************************
***
//*
//STEP1     EXEC PGM=IDCAMS
//FILEIN    DD DSN=DSNAME.TEST.FILE1,DISP=SHR
//FILEOUT   DD DSN=DSNAME.TEST.FILE2,
//             DISP=(NEW,CATLG,DELETE),
//             UNIT=SYSDA,
//             SPACE=(TRK,(5,5),RLSE),
//
RECFM=FB,LRECL=80,BLKSIZE=0,DSORG=PS
//SYSIN     DD *
     REPRO   INFILE(FILEIN)   -
             OUTFILE(FILEOUT) -
             SKIP  (1000) -
             COUNT (500)
//SYSPRINT  DD SYSOUT=*
//SYSUDUMP  DD SYSOUT=*
//
```

Initializing a File to Empty

You can create an empty file by using IDCAMS REPRO function
and providing a dummy input file specification. The BLKSIZE on
input and output must match or you will get an error.

```
//JOB00101 JOB (ACCTCODE),'NAME',
//    CLASS=A,NOTIFY=USERID,MSGCLASS=A
//*
//STEP1     EXEC PGM=IDCAMS
//INFILE    DD DUMMY,
//             BLKSIZE=23250
//OUTFILE   DD DSN=DSNAME.FILE.TEST,
//             DISP=(NEW,CATLG,DELETE),
//             UNIT=TAPE,
//             RECFM=FB,LRECL=250,BLKSIZE=23250
//SYSPRINT  DD SYSOUT=*
//SYSIN     DD *
  REPRO INFILE (INFILE) OUTFILE (OUTFILE)
/*
//
```

Verifying Data Exists in a File

Sometimes you will need to verify whether there is any data in a file. For example, you may have a job that should conditionally process a file depending on whether there is data in the file. One way is to use an IDCAMS read, code a dummy output file, and specify a COUNT of 1. If the file is empty, you will get a 04 return code from IDCAMS. Subsequent job steps can test the return code, and only execute if there is in fact data – for example COND=(0,NE) or (0,LT).

```
//JOB00101 JOB (ACCTCODE),'NAME',
//   CLASS=A,NOTIFY=USERID,MSGCLASS=A
//*
//STEP1     EXEC PGM=IDCAMS
//SYSUDUMP  DD SYSOUT=*
//SYSPRINT  DD SYSOUT=*
//FILEIN    DD DSN=DSNAME.TEST.FILE1,DISP=SHR
//FILEOUT   DD
DUMMY,RECFM=FB,LRECL=80,BLKSIZE=8000
//SYSIN     DD *
      REPRO   INFILE(FILEIN) -
              OUTFILE(FILEOUT) -
              COUNT(1)
/*
//
```

Renaming a File

Since you can generally rename a file online, you might not have many occasions when you need a batch job for this purpose. One possible use is if you have several files to rename as part of a standardization project. In this case you use **ALTER** with **RENAME** to get this result.

```
//JOB00101 JOB (ACCTCODE),'NAME',
//  CLASS=A,NOTIFY=USERID,MSGCLASS=A
//*
//*********************************************
***
//* IDCAMS TO RENAME A DATA SET
//*********************************************
***
//*
//STEP1     EXEC PGM=IDCAMS
//SYSPRINT  DD SYSOUT=*
//SYSUDUMP  DD SYSOUT=*
//SYSIN     DD *
  ALTER DSNAME.TEST.FILE1 -
  NEWNAME(DSNAME.TEST.FILE2)
/*
//
```

Deleting a File

There are many utilities that allow you to delete a file. Here is the IDCAMS function to perform a delete.

```
//JOB00101 JOB (ACCTCODE),'NAME',
//  CLASS=A,MSGCLASS=A,NOTIFY=USERID
//*
//************************************************
***
//*   IDCAMS TO DELETE A DATA SET
//************************************************
***
//*
//STEP1    EXEC PGM=IDCAMS
//SYSPRINT  DD SYSOUT=*
//SYSIN     DD *
 DELETE DSNAME.TEST.FILE
/*
//
```

Building a GDG

Create a GDG base using the **DEFINE GDG** command. NAME is
the dataset name for the base. LIMIT is how many generations.
Normally you should include the SCRATCH parameter so that the
oldest generation gets scratched when the limit is exceeded.

```
//JOB00101 JOB (ACCTCODE),'NAME',
//    CLASS=A,NOTIFY=YOURID,MSGCLASS=A
//*
//************************************************
***
//*     DEFINE GDG
//************************************************
***
//*
//STEP1     EXEC PGM=IDCAMS
//SYSPRINT  DD SYSOUT=*
//SYSIN     DD *
  DEFINE GDG -
         (NAME(DSNAME.FILEGDG.FILENAME) -
         LIMIT(2) SCRATCH)
/*
//
```

Adjusting the Number of Gens on a GDG

You can change the number of generations on a GDG by using the
ALTER command and the **LIMIT** parameter. You can increase or
decrease the number of gens. This JCL sets the number of gens to 5.
Note that if more than 5 generations are already cataloged, the oldest
will be deleted by the o/s leaving the most recent 5 (provided the
SCRATCH clause was used when the GDG was set up).

```
//JOB001I  JOB (ACCTCODE),'WINGATE- 6510',
//  CLASS=A,NOTIFY=USERID,MSGCLASS=A
//*
//JS001   EXEC PGM=IDCAMS
//SYSPRINT  DD SYSOUT=*
//SYSIN    DD *
 ALTER    DATASET.GDG.BANAME   SCR LIMIT(5)
//*
//
```

Deleting all Generations of a GDG

You may have occasion to delete all gens of a GDG (such as
accumulating several gens, processing them all, and then deleting
them all). The following JCL will delete all generations of a GDG
by using a wild card (*) as the last node of the file name to delete (the
G00 part). The GDG base will remain and the next generation
created will be G0001V00. .

```
//JOB001ID JOB (ACCTCODE),'WINGATE- 6510 ',
//   CLASS=A,MSGCLASS=A,NOTIFY=USERID
//*
//************************************************
***
//*    IDCAMS TO DELETE ALL GENS OF A GDG
//************************************************
***
//*
//STEP1     EXEC PGM=IDCAMS
//SYSPRINT  DD SYSOUT=*
//SYSIN     DD *
 DELETE DSNAME.FILEGDG.FILENAME.*
/*
//
```

Deleting an Entire GDG and Index

You may have occasion to completely delete and "un-define" a GDG, such as if you are cleaning up or standardizing file names. The following JCL will delete all generations of a GDG and then remove the base definition from the system. Note the use of the GDG and FORCE parameters. FORCE is what causes existing generations of the GDG to be deleted.

```
//JOB001GP JOB (ACCTCODE),'NAME',
//      CLASS=A,MSGCLASS=A,NOTIFY=USERID
//*
//************************************************
***
//*  DELETE GDG INDEX AND ALL ENTRIES
*
//************************************************
***
//*
//STEP1    EXEC PGM=IDCAMS
//SYSPRINT  DD SYSOUT=*
//SYSIN     DD *
    DELETE DSNAME.TEST.FILEX GDG FORCE
/*
//
```

Listing Catalog Entries

When you want a listing of catalog information about a dataset, use the LISTCAT command. The following provides catalog information about a GDG whose base name is DSNAME.GDGFILE.TEST1.

```
//JOB001LC   JOB (ACCTCODE),'NAME',
//  CLASS=B,NOTIFY=USERID,MSGCLASS=A
//*
//STEP1     EXEC PGM=IDCAMS
//SYSPRINT  DD SYSOUT=X
//SYSIN     DD *
 LISTCAT GDG ENT('DSNAME.GDGFILE.TEST1') ALL
/*
//
```

Printing a File

Several IBM utilities allow you to print a file. Here is the IDCAMS print command. In this case, we are requesting character format.

```
//JOB001IP JOB (ACCTCODE),'NAME',
//  CLASS=A,MSGCLASS=A,NOTIFY=USERID
//*
//************************************************
***
//*   IDCAMS TO PRINT A DATA SET
//************************************************
***
//*
//STEP1     EXEC PGM=IDCAMS
//SYSPRINT  DD SYSOUT=*
//FILEIN    DD DSN=DSNAME.TEST.FILE,
//             DISP=SHR
//SYSIN     DD *
 PRINT INFILE (FILEIN) CHAR
/*
//
```

Printing a File Dump

Use this JCL if you need a hex dump of a file. It may be useful when you are diagnosing a problem, such as a data related abend where a simple character print does not show you the exact value.

```
//JOB001IP JOB (ACCTCODE),'NAME',
//  CLASS=A,MSGCLASS=A,NOTIFY=USERID
//*
//************************************************
***
//*    IDCAMS TO PRINT A HEX DUMP OF A FILE
//************************************************
***
//*
//STEP1     EXEC PGM=IDCAMS
//SYSPRINT  DD SYSOUT=*
//FILEIN    DD DSN=DSNAME.TEST.FILE,
//             DISP=SHR
//SYSIN     DD *
 PRINT INFILE (FILEIN) -
      DUMP
/*
//
```

IEBCOMPR
Compare Two Sequential Datasets

Often you need to compare two files for difference. An example is if you're performing a regression test, and you want to make sure your baseline and test files are identical. The following provides the compare function. A zero return code means the files are identical. A non-zero RC means the files are not identical.

```
//JOB001IC JOB (ACCTCODE),'NAME',
//  CLASS=A,MSGCLASS=A,NOTIFY=USERID
//************************************************
//*    COMPARE TWO DATASETS
//************************************************
//*
//STEP1    EXEC PGM=IEBCOMPR
//SYSUT1     DD DSN=DSNAME.TEST.FILE1,DISP=SHR
//SYSUT2     DD DSN=DSNAME.TEST.FILE2,DISP=SHR
//SYSIN      DD DUMMY
//SYSPRINT DD SYSOUT=*
//SYSUDUMP DD SYSOUT=*
//
```

Compare Two Partitioned Datasets

This example works the same as the above – the only difference is that we are comparing partitioned data sets.

```
//JOB001IC JOB (ACCTCODE),'NAME',
//  CLASS=A,MSGCLASS=A,NOTIFY=USERID
//***********************************************
***
//*    COMPARE TWO DATASETS
//***********************************************
***
//*
//STEP1     EXEC PGM=IEBCOMPR
//SYSPRINT DD SYSOUT=A
//SYSUT1    DD DSN=DSNAME.TEST.PDSFILE1,DISP=SHR
//SYSUT2    DD DSN=DSNAME.TEST.PDSFILE2,DISP=SHR
//SYSIN     DD  *
   COMPARE   TYPORG=PO
/*
//
```

IEBGENER
Copying a File

IEBGENER is one of the most used MVS utilities. Typically it is
used to copy or print a file, although it can also be used to edit a file.
Here is the JCL for a plain vanilla copy. You must specify **SYSUT1**
and **SYSUT2** as the original and new file respectively. Specifying
SYSIN as a dummy dataset means that IEBGENER will perform its
default action, which is to copy SYSUT1 to SYSUT2.

```
//JOB001GN JOB (ACCTCODE),'NAME',
//  CLASS=A,NOTIFY=USERID,MSGCLASS=A
//*
//STEP1     EXEC PGM=IEBGENER
//SYSUT1    DD DSN=DSNAME.TEST.FILE1,
//             DISP=SHR
//SYSUT2    DD DSN=DSNAME.TEST.FILE2,
//             DISP=(NEW,CATLG,DELETE),
//             UNIT=SYSDA,
//             SPACE=(TRK,(5,5),RLSE),
//
RECFM=FB,LRECL=80,BLKSIZE=0,DSORG=PS
//SYSPRINT  DD SYSOUT=*
//SYSUDUMP  DD DUMMY
//SYSIN     DD DUMMY
//
```

Print a File

To print a file, just use IEBGENER and make sure SYSUT2 specifies a valid print class.

```
//JOB001GN JOB (ACCTCODE),'NAME',
//  CLASS=A,NOTIFY=USERID,MSGCLASS=A
//*
//STEP1    EXEC PGM=IEBGENER
//SYSUT1   DD DSN=DSNAME.TEST.FILE1,
//            DISP=SHR
//SYSUT2   DD SYSOUT=A
//SYSPRINT DD SYSOUT=*
//SYSUDUMP DD DUMMY
//SYSIN    DD DUMMY
//
```

Editing a File - Reformatting

IEBGENER provides a facility for editing a file, although the commands are a bit cryptic. This example reformats a file. That's basically what this "editing" feature is good for: it can save you from having to write and compile a separate program to do a fairly simple edit.

The **GENERATE** and **RECORD FIELD** parameters are mandatory. **MAXFLDS** defines the total number of fields you will specify.
MAXLITS specifies the total field length of fields for which we use literals.

IMPORTANT: Remember that on each FIELD parameter, the first numeric value is the **length** of the field you want to manipulate. The second value is either a literal or else the **starting position** of the data field you want to reference. The last number is the **target displacement** (position) to which you want to put the referenced data. Once you have these three values down, this is a very easy utility to use.

In this case, we are reformatting an 60-byte record by adding a literal "ABCD" as the first 4 bytes of the new file, and then taking the first 44 bytes of the original file and applying them to positions 5 through 48 of the new file. Finally, we pad the last 12 bytes of each record with blanks.

```
//JOB001GN JOB (ACCTCODE),'NAME',
//  CLASS=A,NOTIFY=USERID,MSGCLASS=A
//*
//STEP1     EXEC PGM=IEBGENER
//SYSUT1    DD DSN=DSNAME.TEST.FILE1,DISP=SHR
//SYSUT2    DD DSN=DSNAME.TEST.FILE2,
//             DISP=(NEW,CATLG,DELETE),
//             UNIT=SYSDA,
//             SPACE=(TRK,(5,5),RLSE),
//
RECFM=FB,LRECL=60,BLKSIZE=0,DSORG=PS
//SYSPRINT  DD SYSOUT=*
//SYSUDUMP  DD DUMMY
//SYSIN     DD *
          GENERATE MAXFLDS=4,MAXLITS=40
      RECORD FIELD=(4,'ABCD',,1),
             FIELD=(44,1,,5),
             FIELD=(12,'"            ',,49)
/*
//
```

IEBCOPY

Copying a Partitioned Dataset

You will typically use IEBCOPY to make a copy of a partitioned dataset. It is most useful for backing up or restoring a PDS. You can specify the input and output DDNAMEs in the COPY statement.

```
//JOB001C2 JOB (ACCTCODE),'NAME',
//    CLASS=A,MSGCLASS=A,NOTIFY=USERID
//************************************************
***
//*    COPY A PARTITIONED DS
//************************************************
***
//*
//STEP1     EXEC PGM=IEBCOPY
//SYSIN     DD *
  COPY INDD=SYSUT1,OUTDD=SYSUT2
/*
//SYSUT1    DD DSN=DSNAME.PDS.FILE,DISP=SHR
//SYSUT2    DD DSN=DSNAME.PDS.FILE.BACKUP,
//             DISP=(NEW,CATLG,DELETE),
//             UNIT=TAPE,RECFM=FB,LRECL=80,
//             DSORG=PO,BLKSIZE=27920
//SYSUT3    DD UNIT=SYSDA,
//             SPACE=(TRK,(100,100),RLSE)
//SYSUT4    DD UNIT=SYSDA,
//             SPACE=(TRK,(100,100),RLSE)
//SYSPRINT  DD SYSOUT=*
//SYSUDUMP  DD SYSOUT=*
//
```

Copying Specific Members of a PDS

You can also use IEBCOPY to copy a subset of an original PDS. To do this, use the SELECT MEMBER option. The following JCL specifies four members of a PDS to be copied.

```
//JOB001C2 JOB (ACCTCODE),'NAME',
//       CLASS=A,MSGCLASS=A,NOTIFY=USERID
//**********************************************
***
//*   COPY MEMBERS OF A PDS TO ANOTHER PDS
//**********************************************
***
//*
//STEP1     EXEC PGM=IEBCOPY
//SYSIN     DD *
  COPY INDD=SYSUT1,OUTDD=SYSUT2
  SELECT MEMBER=(MEMBER1,MEMBER2,MEMBER3,MEMBER4)
//*
//SYSUT1    DD DSN=DSNAME.PDS.FILE,DISP=SHR
//SYSUT2    DD DSN=DSNAME.PDS.NEWFILE,
//             DISP=(NEW,CATLG,DELETE),
//             UNIT=SYSDA,
//             SPACE=(TRK,(20,20,10),RLSE),
//
RECFM=FB,LRECL=80,DSORG=PO,BLKSIZE=27920
//SYSUT3    DD UNIT=SYSDA,
//             SPACE=(TRK,(60,90),RLSE)
//SYSUT4    DD UNIT=SYSDA,
//             SPACE=(TRK,(60,90),RLSE)
//SYSPRINT  DD SYSOUT=*
//SYSUDUMP  DD SYSOUT=*
//
```

Compressing a PDS

You can also use IEBCOPY to compress the space used by a PDS.
To do this, simply specify the input and output dataset as the same
name. The following JCL shows this technique.

```
//JOB001C2 JOB (ACCTCODE),'NAME',
//       CLASS=A,MSGCLASS=A,NOTIFY=USERID
//************************************************
***
//*    COPY MEMBERS OF A PDS TO ANOTHER PDS
//************************************************
***
//*
//STEP1    EXEC PGM=IEBCOPY
//SYSIN    DD *
  COPY INDD=SYSUT1,OUTDD=SYSUT2
//*
//SYSUT1    DD DSN=DSNAME.PDS.FILE,DISP=OLD
//SYSUT2    DD DSN=DSNAME.PDS.FILE,DISP=OLD
//SYSPRINT  DD SYSOUT=*
//SYSUDUMP  DD SYSOUT=*
//
```

IEFBR14

IEFBR14 has a variety of uses. Most often it is used to delete a file.

The following deletes the referenced data sets. Also, by specifying (MOD,DELETE,DELETE) as the disposition, IEFBR14 first creates the catalog entry for the files if they do not exist. Why do it this way? Because it is flexible, allowing for the possibility that the files to be deleted do not actually exist every time the job runs. If the files do exist, they get deleted. If they do not exist, you prevent a runtime error (trying to delete a non-existent file) by specifying MOD as the first sub-parameter of the disposition.

Deleting a File

```
//JOB001IF JOB (ACCTCODE),'NAME',
//   CLASS=A,NOTIFY=USERID,MSGCLASS=A
//*
//STEP1     EXEC PGM=IEFBR14
//DD1       DD DSN=DSNAME.TEST.FILE1,
//             DISP=(MOD,DELETE,DELETE),
//             UNIT=SYSDA,SPACE=(TRK,(0,0),RLSE)
//SYSPRINT  DD SYSOUT=*
//SYSUDUMP  DD SYSOUT=*
//
```

IEHLIST
Listing Dataset Information for a Volume

In some cases, you may wish to obtain dataset information about a particular DASD volume. Use IEHLIST with the LISTVTOC command to obtain this information. VOLNAME1 refers to the actual volume name.

```
//JOB001I  JOB (ACCTCODE),'NAME',
//  CLASS=A,NOTIFY=USERID,MSGCLASS=A
//*
//STEP1     EXEC PGM=IEHLIST
//SYSPRINT  DD SYSOUT=*
//SYSUDUMP  DD SYSOUT=*
//DD1       DD
UNIT=SYSDA,VOL=SER=VOLNAME1,DISP=SHR
//SYSIN     DD *
  LISTVTOC VOL=SYSDA=VOLNAME1,FORMAT
```

Listing Dataset Information for a PDS

In addition to volume information, you can get detailed information about a partitioned dataset by using IEHLIST with the LISTPDS option. This JCL shows how to do this.

```
//JOB001LP JOB (ACCTCODE),'NAME',
//  CLASS=A,NOTIFY=USERID,MSGCLASS=A
//*
//STEP1     EXEC PGM=IEHLIST
//SYSPRINT  DD SYSOUT=*
//SYSUDUMP  DD SYSOUT=*
//DD1       DD
UNIT=SYSALLDA,VOL=SER=VOLNAME,DISP=SHR
//SYSIN     DD *
  LISTPDS
DSNAME=PDS.FILE.NAME,VOL=SYSALLDA=VOLNAME,FORMAT
//
```

SYNCSORT
Copying a File

SORT is a very common and efficient utility for copying large files. It also has other features that make it more flexible for file manipulation than IEBGENER or IDCAMS. SORT is often the tool of choice for many file operations. The following example does a simple file copy. SORTIN and SORTOUT are always the DDNAMEs for the input and output files respectively.

```
//JOB001SS JOB (ACCTCODE),'NAME',
//   CLASS=A,NOTIFY=USERID,MSGCLASS=A
//*
//************************************************
***
//*      DO A SIMPLE COPY OF A FILE USING SORT
//************************************************
***
//*
//STEP1     EXEC PGM=SORT
//SORTIN    DD DSN=DSNAME.TEST.FILE1,DISP=SHR
//SORTOUT   DD DSN=DSNAME.TEST.FILE2,
//             DISP=(NEW,CATLG,DELETE),
//             UNIT=SYSDA,
//             SPACE=(TRK,(5,5),RLSE),
//
RECFM=FB,LRECL=80,BLKSIZE=0,DSORG=PS
//SORTWK01  DD UNIT=SYSDA,
//             SPACE=(TRK,(5,5),RLSE)
//SORTWK02  DD UNIT=SYSDA,
//             SPACE=(TRK,(5,5),RLSE)
//SYSIN     DD *
  SORT FIELDS=COPY
//SYSOUT    DD SYSOUT=*
//SYSPRINT  DD SYSOUT=*
//
```

Sorting a File

Naturally, the SORT utility can be used for sorting a file. The following example shows the syntax. In this case, it sorts a file into ascending sequence based on positions 1 through 4 of the file, and within that major order, it sorts in descending sequence according to the packed decimal values in positions 12 through 14.

```
//JOB001SS JOB (ACCTCODE),'NAME',CLASS=A,
// NOTIFY=USERID,MSGCLASS=A
//********************************************
***
//* SORT - USE POSITIONS 1-4 ASCENDING AS PRIMARY
//* SORTKEY, AND 12-14 DESCENDING AS SECONDARY
KEY
//********************************************
***
//STEP1     EXEC PGM=SORT
//SYSOUT    DD SYSOUT=X
//SORTIN    DD DSN=DSNAME.FILE.TOSORT,DISP=SHR
//SORTOUT   DD DSN=DSNAME.FILE.SORTED,
//             DISP=(NEW,CATLG,DELETE),
//             UNIT=TAPE,
//             RECFM=FB,BLKSIZE=8160,LRECL=20
//SORTWK01  DD UNIT=SYSDA,
//             SPACE=(TRK,(90,9),RLSE)
//SORTWK02  DD UNIT=SYSDA,
//             SPACE=(TRK,(9000,900),RLSE)
//SYSIN     DD *
  SORT FIELDS=(1,4,CH,A,12,3,PD,D)
 END
 /*
//
```

Sorting Out Selected Records

Sometimes you may need to strip certain records from a file. Here are two samples of what you can do with SORT. In the first example, only records with a "Z" value in position one will be written to the SORTOUT file. The second example shows only a control card, and the point is to show an example of multiple select conditions.

Single Select Condition

```
//JOB001SS JOB (ACCTCODE),'NAME',
//   CLASS=A,NOTIFY=USERID,MSGCLASS=A
//************************************************
***
//*   SORT OUT RECORDS BASED UPON CRITERIA
//************************************************
***
//*
//STEP1     EXEC PGM=SORT
//SORTIN    DD DSN=DSNAME.FILE.TESTIN,DISP=SHR
//SORTOUT   DD DSN=DSNAME.FILE.TESTOUT,
//             DISP=(NEW,CATLG,DELETE),
//             UNIT=SYSDA,
//             SPACE=(TRK,(60,10),RLSE),
//
LRECL=250,BLKSIZE=0,RECFM=FB,DSORG=PS
//SORTWK01  DD UNIT=SYSDA,
//             SPACE=(TRK,(50,50),RLSE)
//SORTWK02  DD UNIT=SYSDA,
//             SPACE=(TRK,(50,50),RLSE)
//SYSOUT    DD SYSOUT=*
//SYSPRINT  DD SYSOUT=*
   SORT FIELDS=COPY
   INCLUDE COND=(1,1,CH,EQ,C'Z')
   OUTREC FIELDS=(1,250)
 END
//*
//
```

Multiple Select Condition

Here is what a control card would look like to select all records for which the first character is "Z" and characters 40-41 are NOT "AA".

```
SORT FIELDS=COPY
INCLUDE COND=(1,1,CH,EQ,C'Z',AND,
             40,2,CH,NE,C'AA')
```

As you probably guessed, the Booleans for comparison are "EQ" for equal, "NE" for not equal, etc. Check the references if you need full documentation.

Omitting Selected Records

Sometimes you may need to remove certain records from a file. Here are two samples of how you can do that, and it is exactly the opposite of the INCLUDE examples. In the first example, records with a "Z" value in position one will be omitted from the SORTOUT file. The second example shows only a control card, and the point is to show an example of multiple OMIT conditions.

Single OMIT Condition

```
//JOB001SS JOB (ACCTCODE),'NAME',
//  CLASS=A,NOTIFY=USERID,MSGCLASS=A
//*********************************************
***
//*  SORT OUT RECORDS BASED UPON CRITERIA
//*********************************************
***
//*
//STEP1     EXEC PGM=SORT
//SORTIN    DD DSN=DSNAME.FILE.TESTIN,DISP=SHR
//SORTOUT   DD DSN=DSNAME.FILE.TESTOUT,
//             DISP=(NEW,CATLG,DELETE),
//             UNIT=SYSDA,
//             SPACE=(TRK,(60,10),RLSE),
//
LRECL=250,BLKSIZE=0,RECFM=FB,DSORG=PS
//SORTWK01  DD UNIT=SYSDA,
//             SPACE=(TRK,(50,50),RLSE)
//SORTWK02  DD UNIT=SYSDA,
//             SPACE=(TRK,(50,50),RLSE)
//SYSOUT    DD SYSOUT=*
//SYSPRINT  DD SYSOUT=*
   SORT FIELDS=COPY
   OMIT COND=(1,1,CH,EQ,C'Z')
   OUTREC FIELDS=(1,250)
 END
//*
//
```

Multiple OMIT Condition

Here is what a control card would look like to OMIT all records for which the first character is "Z" and characters 40-41 are NOT "AA".

```
SORT FIELDS=COPY
OMIT COND=(1,1,CH,EQ,C'Z',AND,
           40,2,CH,NE,C'AA')
```

Note: Besides AND, you can use the Boolean OR condition in establishing multiple conditions for both INCLUDE and OMIT. Just remember what your requirement is and what you intend to do. Oddly, one of the most frequent logic errors I've seen in programming is using one of these where the other is intended.

Sorting Into a Smaller Sized Record

Sometimes you may need to create a new file with a smaller record length than the original. SORT allows you to do this by specifying **OUTREC FIELDS**. The length you specify must match the file parameters on the SORTOUT DD.

In the following example, we have an input file for which the records are 80 bytes long. We extract only positions 1-4, and 40-56 by specifying these as the OUTREC fields. This results in an output file for which the records are 20 positions in length.

```
//JOB001SS JOB (ACCTCODE),'NAME',
//  CLASS=A,NOTIFY=USERID,MSGCLASS=A
//*********************************************
***
//*  SORT OUT RECORDS BASED UPON CRITERIA
//*********************************************
***
//*
//STEP1     EXEC PGM=SORT
//SORTIN    DD DSN=DSNAME.FILEIN,DISP=SHR
//SORTOUT   DD DSN=DSNAME.FILEOUT,
//             DISP=(NEW,CATLG,DELETE),
//             UNIT=SYSDA,
//             SPACE=(TRK,(10,5),RLSE),
//
RECFM=FB,LRECL=20,BLKSIZE=0,DSORG=PS
//SORTWK01  DD
UNIT=SYSDA,SPACE=(TRK,(16,16),RLSE)
//SORTWK02  DD
UNIT=SYSDA,SPACE=(TRK,(16,16),RLSE)
//SYSOUT    DD SYSOUT=*
//SYSIN     DD *
  SORT FIELDS=COPY
  OUTREC FIELDS=(1,4,40,56)
 END
/*
//
```

Removing Duplicate Records

You can remove duplicate records from a file by using the SUM
clause. Whatever you specified as the sort fields will be used to
determine whether a record is a duplicate of another record. The
example removes duplicate records where the "key" is defined as
positions 1-4, and 40-49.

```
//JOB001SR  JOB (ACCTCODE),'NAME',CLASS=A,
//   NOTIFY=USERID,MSGCLASS=A
//*********************************************
***
//*  SORT
//*********************************************
***
//STEP1     EXEC PGM=SORT
//SYSOUT    DD SYSOUT=*
//SYSPRINT  DD SYSOUT=*
//SORTIN    DD DSN=DSNAME.FILEIN,DISP=SHR
//SORTOUT   DD DSN=DSNAME.FILEOUT,
//            DISP=(NEW,CATLG,DELETE),
//            UNIT=SYSDA,
//            SPACE=(TRK,(50,10),RLSE),
//
RECFM=FB,LRECL=250,BLKSIZE=0,DSORG=PS
//SORTWK01  DD UNIT=SYSDA,
//            SPACE=(TRK,(50,10),RLSE)
//SORTWK02  DD UNIT=SYSDA,
//            SPACE=(TRK,(50,10),RLSE)
//SYSIN     DD *
  SORT FIELDS=(1,4,CH,A,40,49,CH,A)
  SUM FIELDS=NONE
 END
 /*
//
```

Removing Unmatched Records

You can do quite a lot with SORT such as creating a file with all matched records from two files, or removing unmatched records from a file. The example I provide here will write a file of records from file 2 that do not exist in file 1. In this case the records with values 234 and 678 in file 2 are not matched to any values in File 1.

The JOINKEYS statements tell us which fields in each file we are comparing. The JOIN UNPAIRED,F2,ONLY means we are only interested in the unpaired records in the second file. REFORMAT tells us which fields we are preserving for output.

```
//JOB001SR  JOB (ACCTCODE),'NAME',CLASS=A,
//   NOTIFY=USERID,MSGCLASS=A
//*************************************************
//*   SORT
//*************************************************
//STEP1     EXEC PGM=SORT
//SYSOUT    DD SYSOUT=*
//SYSPRINT  DD SYSOUT=*
//SORTIN1   DD *
123
456
789
//SORTIN2   DD *
123
234
456
678
789
//SORTOUT   DD DSN=DSNAME.SORTOUT,
//             DISP=(NEW,CATLG,DELETE),
//             UNIT=SYSDA,
//             SPACE=(TRK,(50,10),RLSE),
//             RECFM=FB,LRECL=250,BLKSIZE=0,DSORG=PS
//SYSIN     DD *
//SYSIN     DD *
  JOINKEYS F1=SORTIN1,FIELDS=(1,3,A)
  JOINKEYS F2=SORTIN2,FIELDS=(1,3,A)
  JOIN UNPAIRED,F2,ONLY
  REFORMAT FIELDS=(F2:1,3)
  SORT FIELDS=(1,3,CH,A)
/*
```

SUPERC

SUPERC is a handy file comparison utility that is often invoked online but has a batch option as well. If you specify batch mode using the online utility you can capture the JCL and subsequently run it yourself. The JCL looks like the following. OLDDD and NEWDD are the DDNAMEs for the datasets to be compared.

Comparing the Contents of Two Files

You compare the contents of two files as follows:

```
//JOB001B  JOB  (ACCTCODE),'PROGRAMMER',
//    CLASS=A,MSGCLASS=A,NOTIFY=USERID
//*
//STEP1 EXEC PGM=ISRSUPC,
//            PARM=(CHNGL,LINECMP,
//              '',
//              ''))
//NEWDD   DD DSN=PDSFILE1(MEMBER1),
//            DISP=SHR
//OLDDD   DD DSN=PDSFILE2(MEMBER),
//            DISP=SHR
//OUTDD   DD SYSOUT=*
```

Searching a Dataset for a String Value

You can search a file for a particular string s follows:

```
//JOB001W  JOB
ACCTCODE),'PROGRAMMER',CLASS=A,MSGCLASS=A,
//         NOTIFY=USERID
//*
//SEARCH  EXEC PGM=ISRSUPC,
*
//             PARM=(SRCHCMP,
//              '')
//NEWDD  DD DSN=FILE.TO.BE.SEARCHD,
//         DISP=SHR
//OUTDD  DD SYSOUT=(X)
//SYSIN  DD *
SRCHFOR  'STRING VALUE I AM LOOKING FOR'
/*
//
```

Appendix A – Web Resources

Add some MVS web resources

http://www.theamericanprogrammer.com/programming/manuals.jcl.shtml

http://www.mvshelp.com

http://www.ibmmainframes.com/manuals.php

http://www.exforsys.com/tutorials/mainframe/introduction-to-jcl.html